with the band

Yarn

Sheep(ish) by Vickie Howell by Bernat 3oz/85g skeins, each approx 167yd/153m (acrylic/wool) 2 skeins,

- 1 each in Grey(ish) #0003 (A) and Yellow(ish) #0012 (B)

Needles

Size H/8 (5.0mm) crochet hook OR SIZE NEEDED TO OBTAIN GAUGE

Additional

Tapestry needle
1" button in coordinating color
Sewing needle and thread to attach button

Measurements

3½"/9cm x 18"/45.75cm excluding button loop

Gauge

12 sts and 10 rows to 4"/10cm over hdc
TAKE TIME TO CHECK YOUR GAUGE.

Note

Ch-2 does not count as 1 hdc

Directions (Make 2)

With A, ch 15.

Row 1 2 Hdc in 3rd ch from hook, hdc in each of next 4 ch, sk 2 ch, hdc in each of next 4 ch, 2 hdc in last ch. Ch 2, turn. 12 hdc; t-ch does not count as hdc

Row 2 2 hdc in 1st hdc, hdc in each of next 4 hdc, sk 2 hdc, hdc in each of next 4 hdc, 2 hdc in last hdc. Ch 2, turn.

Row 3 Rep Row 2.

Row 4 Rep Row 2, end off A, ch 2 turn in B.

Rows 5-7 Rep Row 2.

Row 8 Rep Row 2, end off B, ch 2 turn in A.

Rows 9-12 Rep Row 2.

Row 13 Hdc in each of next 5 hdc, dc in each of next 2 hdc, hdc in each of next 5 hdc. End off.

Finishing

Whip st 2 pieces together at straight edges.

Edging

With A, work 1 rnd hdc evenly spaced around assembled piece, working 3 hdc at each corner and point. End off.

Button Loop

Join A with sl st at either point. Ch 13, sl st in 6th ch from hook, ch 7, sl st in original point. End off.

Sew button onto opposite point.

Weave in ends. Block if necessary.

magenta lane

Yarn ④

Sheep(ish) by Vickie Howell by Bernat
3oz/85g skeins, each approx 167yd/153m
(acrylic/wool)

• 1 skein Magenta(ish) #0006

Needles

Size I/9 (5.5mm) crochet hook OR SIZE
NEEDED TO OBTAIN GAUGE

Additional

Tapestry needle

Measurements

11"/28 cm tall x 22"/56cm in diameter,
slightly stretched

Gauge

10 sts x 8 rows = 4"/10 cm over
FP/BPhdc Rib
TAKE TIME TO CHECK YOUR GAUGE.

Notes

Ch-2 does not count as 1 hdc
Ch-3 counts as 1 dc throughout

Stitch Glossary

Shell = (2 tr, ch 1, 2 tr, ch 1, 2 tr) in
specified st
FPhdc = front post half double crochet
BPhdc = back post half double crochet
Hdc2tog = half double crochet 2 sts
together

Directions

Body

Ch 50. Join into ring with sl st in 1st ch,
taking care not to twist.

Rnd 1 Ch 3 (counts as 1 dc here and
throughout), dc in same ch as sl st, (sk 1
ch, 2 dc in next ch) twice, ch 2, sk 2 ch, (sc,
ch 2, sc) in next ch, ch 2, *sk 2 ch, 2 dc in
next ch, (sk 1 ch, 2 dc in next ch) twice, ch
2, (sc, ch 2, sc) in next ch, ch 2. Rep from *
around. Join rnd with sl st in top of beg-ch.
5 dc groups + 15 ch-2 sps

Rnd 2 Ch 3, (2 dc between 2nd and 3rd dc
from hook) twice, sk next ch-2 sp, shell in
next ch-2 sp, *(2 dc between 2nd and 3rd
ch from hook) 3 times, sk next ch-2 sp,
shell in next ch-2 sp. Rep from * around, dc
in same sp as 1st sl st. Join rnd with a sl st
in top of beg-ch.

Rnd 3 Ch 3, (2 dc between 2nd and 3rd dc
from hook) twice, ch 2, (sc in next ch-1 sp,
ch 2) twice, *(2 dc between 2nd and 3rd
ch from hook) 3 times, ch 2, (sc in next
ch-1 sp, ch 2) twice. Rep from * across dc
in same sp as 1st sl st. Join rnd with sl st in
top of beg-ch.

Rnds 4-12 Rep Rnds 2 & 3 4 more times
then Rnd 2 once more.

Rnd 13 Ch 2 (does not count as hdc), hdc
in each dc and tr around. Join rnd with sl st
in top of beg-ch. 60 hdc

Rnd 14 Ch 2, hdc in each hdc around
working 12 decs evenly spaced. 48 hdc

Brim

Rnds 1-4 Ch 2, *FPhdc, BPhdc; rep from *
around. Join rnd with sl st in top of beg-ch.

End off.

Finishing

Close Top of Hat At top of hat, join yarn
with sc, inserting hook through center front
and center back (joining front and back
at center). Pinch side edges to the same
center point and sc the edges together by
inserting hook through both thicknesses
and completing a sc. The top of the beanie
will now be in a star formation. Continue to
pinch opposite edges and sc them together
until top of beanie is completely closed.
End off.

Weave in ends.

tangerine dream

Yarn (4)

Sheep(ish) by Vickie Howell by Bernat
3oz/85g skeins, each approx 167yd/153m
(acrylic/wool)
• 2 skeins Coral(ish) #0014

Needles

Size H/8 (5.0mm) crochet hook OR SIZE
NEEDED TO OBTAIN GAUGE

Additional

Tapestry needle

Measurements

11"/28 cm tall x 22"/56 cm in diameter
slightly stretched

Gauge

12 sts and 10 rows to 4"/10cm over hdc
TAKE TIME TO CHECK YOUR GAUGE.

Notes

Ch-2 does not count as 1 hdc

Stitch Glossary

FPtr = front post triple crochet
FPhdc = front post half double crochet
BPhdc = back post half double crochet

Directions

Body

Ch 64. Join into ring with sl st in 1st ch,
taking care not to twist.
Rnd 1 Ch 2 (does not count as hdc), hdc
in same ch as sl st, and in each ch around.
Join rnd with sl st in top of beg-ch. 64 hdc
Rnd 2 Ch 2, hdc in each hdc around. Join
rnd with sl st in top of beg-ch.
Rnd 3 Ch 2, * hdc in each of next 4 hdc,
FPtr in stitch 2 below each of next 4 hdc
(opposite side of foundation ch). Rep from
* around. Join rnd with sl st in top of beg-
ch. 32 FPtr, 32 hdc
Rnd 4 Ch 2, hdc in each st around. Join rnd
with sl st in top of beg-ch. 64 hdc
Rnd 5 Ch 2, *hdc in each of next 4 hdc, sk
2 sts, FPtr in FPtr below each of next 2 hdc,
FPtr in FPtr below each of 2 skipped hdc.
Rep from * around. Join rnd with sl st in
top of beg-ch.
Rnd 6 Rep Rnd 2.
Rnd 7 Ch 2, * hdc in each of next 4 hdc,
FPtr in FPtr below each of next 4 hdc. Rep
from * around. Join rnd with sl st in top of
beg-ch.

Rnd 8 Rep Rnd 2
Rnd 9 Rep Rnd 7
Rnds 10-13 Rep Rnd 4 - 7
Repeat Rnds 8-13 twice more.

Brim

Rnds 1-4 Ch 2, *FPhdc, BPhdc; rep from
* around. Join rnd with sl st in top of beg-ch

End off after Rnd 4.

Finishing

Close Top of Hat At top of hat, bring
center front and center back of beanie
together. Join yarn with sc, inserting hook
through center front and center back (joining front and back at center). Pinch side
edges to the same center point and sc the
edges together (by inserting hook through
both thicknesses and completing a sc). The
top of the beanie will now be in a star formation. Continue to pinch opposite edges
and sc them together until top of beanie is
completely closed. End off.

Weave in ends.

striped down earflap hat

Yarn 〔4〕
Sheep(ish) by Vickie Howell by Bernat
3oz/85g skeins, each approx 167yd/153m
(acrylic/wool)
• 2 skeins, 1 each in Turquoise(ish)
#0017 (A) and Teal(ish) #0016 (B)

Needles
Size K/10.5 (6.5mm) crochet hook OR
SIZE NEEDED TO OBTAIN GAUGE

Additional
Tapestry needle

Measurements
8"/20cm tall excluding earflap x 22"/56cm
in diameter slightly stretched

Gauge
8 sts and 4 rows to 4"/10cm over dc
TAKE TIME TO CHECK YOUR GAUGE.

Notes
Ch-2 counts as 1 hdc for earflap only, not
on hat body.
Ch-3 does not count as 1 dc.

Yarn is held double throughout. To
double-strand without having to buy additional balls of yarn, simply pull strands
from both the center and outside of 1 ball.
Hold strands together as if they were one.

Stitch Glossary
Hdc2tog = half double crochet 2 stitches
together

Directions
Body
Yarn is held double throughout.
With A, ch 4. Join with sl st in 1st ch to
form ring.
Rnd 1 Ch 3 (doesn't count as st), 12 dc in
center of ring. Join rnd with sl st in top of
beg-ch. 12 dc
Rnd 2 Change to B, ch 3, *2 dc in each dc
around. Join rnd with sl st in top of beg-ch.
24 dc
Rnd 3 Change to A, ch 3, * 2 dc in next dc,
dc in next dc. Rep from * around. 36 dc
Rnd 4 Change to B, ch 3, *2 dc in next dc,
dc in each of next 2 dc. Rep from * around.
48 dc
Rnds 5-8 Continue to alternate colors every
rnd; Ch 3, dc in each dc around.
Rnd 9:Change to A, ch 2, hdc in each dc
around.
End off.

Earflaps
Count 8 sts over from your finishing point.
Join A.
Rows 1 & 2 Ch 2, hdc in each of next 7 hdc.
Turn. 8 hdc counting ch-2 as 1 hdc
Row 3 Ch 2, hdc2tog, hdc in each of next 2
hdc, hdc2tog, hdc in next hdc. Turn. 6 hdc
Row 4 Ch 2, hdc in each of next 5 hdc.
End off.
Repeat on opposite side for 2nd flap WITH-
OUT ending off.

Edging
(RS) Ch 1, sc in each stitch all the way
around hat. End off.

Finishing
Make braids
Cut 9, 30"/76 cm strands of A. Fold strands
in half and attach to ear flap with a knot
by pulling fold through the center edge,
bringing the cut ends through the fold, and
pulling tight. Braid yarn in 3 groups of 6
strands, tie a knot to finish.

Repeat process for opposite side.

Pompom
Using 1 strand each of A & B held together
and 3"/7.5cm piece of cardboard, wrap
yarn around cardboard about 50 times. Slip
wraps off cardboard and tie a piece of yarn
tightly around the center of the wraps. Cut
both ends of wraps and fluff pompom. Trim.
Using beginning and ending tails of tie, tie
pompom to each end.

Weave in ends.

never a skull moment

Yarn [4]

Sheep(ish) by Vickie Howell by Bernat
3oz/85g skeins, each approx 167yd/153m
(acrylic/wool)
• 1 skein Olive(ish) #0019

Needles

Size H/8 (5.0mm) crochet hook OR SIZE
NEEDED TO OBTAIN GAUGE

Additional

Tapestry needle

Measurements

9"/23cm tall x 24"/61cm in diameter,
slightly stretched

Gauge

12 sts and 10 rows to 4"/10cm over hdc
TAKE TIME TO CHECK YOUR GAUGE.

Notes

Ch-2 does not count as hdc

Stitch Glossary

FPhdc= front post half double crochet
BPhdc= back post half double crochet

Directions

Crown

Ch 4. Join into ring with sl st in 1st ch, taking care not to twist.

Rnd 1 Ch 2 (does not count as hdc), 8 hdc into ring. 8 hdc

Rnd 2 Ch 2, 2 hdc in each hdc around. Join rnd with sl st in top of beg-ch. 16 hdc

Rnd 3 Ch 2, *2 hdc in next hdc, hdc in next hdc. Rep from * around. Join rnd with sl st in top of beg-ch. 24 hdc

Rnd 4 Ch 2, * 2 hdc in next hdc, hdc in each of next 2 hdc. Rep from * around. Join rnd with sl st. in top of beg-ch. 32 hdc

Rnd 5 Ch 2, *2 hdc in next hdc, hdc in each of next 3 hdc. Rep from * around. Join rnd with sl st in top of beg-ch. 40 hdc

Rnd 6 Ch 2, *2 hdc in next hdc, hdc in each of next 4 hdc. Rep from * around. Join rnd with sl st in top of beg-ch. 48 hdc

Rnds 7-9 Rep Rnd 6 working 1 additional hdc between 2-hdc increases each rnd. 72 hdc after Rnd 9

Body

Rnds 1-10 Ch 2, hdc in each hdc around. Join rnd with sl st in top of beg-ch. 72 hdc

Rnd 11 Ch 2, hdc in each hdc around to last 2 sts, hdc2tog. 71 hdc

Brim

Rnd 1-3 Ch 2, *FPhdc, Bphdc. Rep from * around. Join with sl st in top of beg-ch.

End off after Rnd 3.

Finishing

Weave in ends.

beret for hollywood

Yarn (4)

Sheep(ish) by Vickie Howell by Bernat
3oz/85g skeins, each approx 167yd/153m
(acrylic/wool)
• 1 skein Chartreuse(ish) #0020

Needles

Size H/8 (5.0mm) crochet hook OR SIZE
NEEDED TO OBTAIN GAUGE

Additional

Tapestry needle

Measurements

11"/25.5cm across top when flat x
22"/56cm in diameter slightly stretched

Gauge

12 sts and 10 rows to 4"/10 cm over hdc
TAKE TIME TO CHECK YOUR GAUGE.

Notes

Ch-7 counts as 1 dc + ch-4
Ch-4 counts as 1 tr
Ch-3 counts as 1 dc unless otherwise noted
Ch-2 does not count as 1 hdc

Stitch Glossary

FPhdc = front post half double crochet
BPhdc = back post half double crochet
dc2tog = double crochet 2 sts together

Directions

Body

Ch 8, join into ring with sl st in 1st ch.

Rnd 1 Ch 7 (counts as 1 dc + ch-4), (dc, ch 4) 5 times in ring. Join rnd with sl st in 3rd ch of beg-ch. 6 ch-4 sps

Rnd 2 Ch 4 (counts as 1 tr here and throughout), *(2 tr, ch 3, 2 tr) in next ch-4 sp, tr in next dc. Rep from * around, omitting last tr. Join rnd with sl st in top of beg-ch. 30 tr

Rnd 3 Sl st across to next ch-3 sp, ch 4, 4 tr in same ch-3 sp, ch 3, sk 2 tr, sc in next tr, ch 3 * 5 tr in next ch-3 sp, ch 3, sk 2 tr, sc in next tr, ch 3. Rep from * around. Join rnd with sl st in top of beg-ch.

Rnd 4 Ch 3 (counts as 1 dc unless otherwise noted), dc in each of next 4 tr, ch 7, *dc in each of next 5 tr, ch 7. Rep from * to end. Join rnd with sl st in top of beg-ch. 30 dc/6 ch-7 sps

Rnd 5 Ch 3, dc in same st, dc in each of next three dc, 2 dc in next dc, 7 dc in ch-7 sp, *2 dc in next dc, dc in each of next 3 dc, 2 dc in next dc, 7 dc in ch-7 sp. Rep from * around Join rnd with sl st in top of beg-ch. 84 dc

Rnd 6 Ch 3, dc in same st as sl st, dc in each of next 4 dc, 2 dc in next dc, dc in each of next 8 dc, * 2 dc in next dc, dc in each of next 4 dc, 2 dc in next dc, dc in each of next 8 dc. Rep from * around. Join rnd with sl st in top of beg-ch. 96 dc

Rnd 7 Ch 3, dc in same st as sl st, dc in each of next 5 dc, 2 dc in next dc, dc in each of next 9 dc, *2 dc in next dc, dc in each of next 5 dc, 2 dc in next dc, dc in each of next 9 dc. Rep from * around. Join rnd with sl st in top of beg-ch. 108 dc

Rnd 8 Ch 3 (does not count as 1 dc), *dc-2tog; rep from * around. Join rnd with sl st in top of beg-ch. 54 sts

Rnds 9-12 Ch 3 (count as 1 dc), dc in each dc around. Join rnd with sl st in top of beg-ch.

Brim

Rnds 1-3: Ch 2 (does not count as 1 hdc), * FPhdc, Bphdc. Rep from * around. Join rnd with sl st in top of beg-ch.

End off.

Finishing

Weave in ends.

granny central station

Yarn (4)

Sheep(ish) by Vickie Howell by Bernat
3oz/85g skeins, each approx 167yd/153m
(acrylic/wool)

- 1 skeins, 1 each in White(ish) #0004
  (A) Yellow(ish) #0012 (B) and
  Red(ish) #0015 (C)

Needles

Size H/8 (5.0mm) crochet hook OR SIZE
NEEDED TO OBTAIN GAUGE

Additional

Tapestry needle

Measurements

10"/25.5cm tall excluding pom pom x
22"/56cm in diameter slightly stretched

Gauge

12 sts and 10 rows to 4"/10cm over dc
TAKE TIME TO CHECK YOUR GAUGE.

Notes

Ch-2 does not count as 1 hdc
Ch-3 counts as 1 dc
Ch-5 counts as 1 dc + ch-2

Stitch Glossary

FPhdc = front post half double crochet
BPhdc = back post half double crochet

Directions

Granny squares (Make 14)

With B, ch 4. Join into ring with sl st in 1st ch.
Rnd 1 Ch 3 (counts as 1 dc here and
throughout), 2 dc in ring, ch 3, (3 dc in
ring, ch 3) 3 times. Join rnd with sl st in top
of beg-ch. 12 dc/4 ch-3 sp
Rnd 2 Change to C, ch 5 (counts as dc +
ch-2), *(3dc, ch 3, 3 dc) in next ch-3 sp, ch
2. rep from * twice more, (3dc, ch 3, 2dc)
in next ch-3 sp, join rnd with sl st in top of
beg-ch. 24 dc/4 ch-3 sp
Rnd 3 Change to A, ch 1, sc in same st as
sl st, 2 sc in next ch-2 sp, sc in each of next
3 dc, 3 sc in ch-3 sp, * sc in each of next 3
dc, 2 sc in ch-2 sp, sc in each of next 3 sc, 3
sc in ch-3 sp. Rep from * twice more, sc in
each of next 2 dc. Join rnd with sl st in 1st
sc. End off. 44 sc

Assembly

Arrange granny squares with RS facing
up into 2 strips of 7 squares each. Using
tapestry needle, sew squares together to
form strips using mattress st. Sew long
edges of strips together. Sew short ends of
assembled piece together to form ring of

squares which will be the hat body.

Band

Join A at bottom of body with sl st in any st.
Rnd 1 Ch 2 (doesn't count as hdc), hdc 54
evenly spaced around. 54 sts
Rnds 2-4 Ch 2, * FPhdc, BPhdc; rep from
* around Join rnd with sl st in top of beg-ch.
End off.

Crown

Join A at top of body with sl st in any st.
Rnd 1 Ch 3, dc 54 evenly spaced around.
Join rnd with sl st in top of beg-ch.54 sts
Rnd 2 & 3 Ch 3, dc in each dc around. Join
rnd with sl st in topof beg-ch.

End off.

Finishing

Close Top of Hat At top of hat, bring
center front and center back of beanie
together. Join yarn with sc, inserting hook
through center front and center back to
join. Pinch side edges to the same center
point and sc the edges together by inserting
hook through both thicknesses and completing a sc. The top of the beanie will now
be in a star formation. Continue to pinch
opposite edges and sc them together until
top of beanie is completely closed. End off.

Pompom
Using A and 3"/7.5cm piece of cardboard,
wrap yarn around cardboard about 50
times. Slip wraps off cardboard and tie a
piece of yarn tightly around the center of
the wraps. Cut both ends of wraps and fluff
pompom. Trim.

Using beginning and ending tails of tie, tie
pompom in place.

Weave in ends.

minty fresh

Yarn (4)

Sheep(ish) by Vickie Howell by Bernat
3oz/85g skeins, each approx 167yd/153m
(acrylic/wool)
- 2 skeins, 1 each in Robin's Egg(ish)
  #0018 (A) and Lime(ish) #0021 (B)

Needles

Size H/8 (5.0mm) crochet hook OR SIZE
NEEDED TO OBTAIN GAUGE

Additional

Stitch marker
Tapestry needle
2 ¾" buttons
Sewing needle and coordinating thread to
attach buttons

Measurements

9"/23cm tall x 22"/56cm in diameter
slightly stretched

Gauge

12 sts and 10 rows to 4"/10cm over hdc
TAKE TIME TO CHECK YOUR GAUGE.

Notes

Ch-2 does not count as 1 hdc in Crown, it
does count as 1 hdc in Band
Ch-3 does not count as 1 dc

Yarn is held double throughout. To
double-strand without having to buy
additional balls of yarn, simply pull
strands from both the center and outside
of 1 ball. Hold strands together as if they
were one.

Stitch Glossary

FPhdc = front post half double crochet
BPhdc = back post half double crochet
Hdc2tog = half double crochet 2 stitches
together

Directions

Crown

With A, ch 4. Join into ring with sl st in 1st
ch, taking care not to twist.

Rnd 1 Ch 2 (does not count as st), 8 hdc
into ring. 8 hdc

Rnd 2 Ch 2, 2 hdc in each hdc around. Join
rnd with sl st. in top of beg-ch. 16 hdc

Rnd 3 Ch 2, *2 hdc in next hdc, hed in next
hdc. Rep from * around. Join rnd with sl st
in top of beg-ch. 24 hdc

Rnd 4 Ch 2, * 2 hdc in next hdc, hdc in
each of next 2 hdc. Rep from * around. Join
rnd with sl st at top of beg-ch. 32 hdc

Rnd 5 Ch 2, * 2 hdc in next hdc, hdc in
each of next 3 hdc. Rep from * around. Join
rnd with sl st. at top of beg-ch. 40 sts

Rnd 6 – 8 Rep Rnd 5 working 1 additional
hdc between 2-hdc increases for every
round.

Continue in this manner working an additional hdc in between "hdc twice" increases,
every round three more times, only on the
last rnd ending with one less hdc on last
repeat. 64 hdc

Rnd 9 With B (do not cut A)*sc in next
st, dc in next st. Rep from * around. Do not
join rnd, mark 1st st and move marker for
each rnd.

Rnd 10 With A, *dc in next st, sc in next st;
repeat from * around.

Rnds 11 – 16 Rep Rnds 9 and 10.
End off both colors.

Band

With B, Ch 11.

Row 1 Hdc in 3rd ch from hook and in each
ch across. Ch 2, turn. 9 hdc counting ch-2

Row 2 Hdcflo across. Ch 2, turn.
Repeat Row 2 until piece measures
21"/53.25 cm.

Next Row Hdc2tog, hdc to last 3 sts, hdc-
2tog, hdc. 7 hdc
Repeat last row twice more. 3 hdc
End off.

Finishing

With 1 strand of Color B and tapestry
needle using the mattress stitch, sew band
to beanie edge. Overlap excess and sew
down.

Weave in ends.

Sew on buttons.

net à porter

Yarn [4]
Sheep(ish) by Vickie Howell by Bernat
3oz/85g skeins, each approx 167yd/153m
(acrylic/wool)
• 1 skein in Hot Pink(ish) #0007

Needles
Size H/8 (5.0mm) crochet hook OR SIZE
NEEDED TO OBTAIN GAUGE

Additional
Tapestry needle

Measurements
8"/20cm tall x 22"/456cm in diameter
slightly stretched

Gauge
12 sts and 10 rows to 4"/10cm over hdc
TAKE TIME TO CHECK YOUR GAUGE.

Notes
Ch-3 counts as 1 dc
Ch-5 counts as 1 dc + ch-2
Ch-6 counts as 1 dc + ch-3
Ch-2 may or may not count as 1 hdc,
details in pattern

Stitch Glossary
FPhdc = front post half double crochet
BPhdc = back post half double crochet

Directions

Crown
Ch 6, join into ring with sl st in 1st ch.
Rnd 1 Ch 3 (counts as 1 dc here and
throughout), 14 dc into ring. Join rnd with
sl st in top of beg-ch. 15 dc
Rnd 2 Ch 5 (counts as 1 dc + ch-2 here and
throughout), *dc in next dc, ch 2. Rep from
* around. Join rnd with sl st in 3rd ch of
beg-ch. 15 ch-2 sps
Rnd 3 Ch 6 (counts as 1 dc + ch-3) *dc in
next dc, ch 3. Rep from * around. Join rnd
with sl st in 3rd ch of beg-ch.
Rnd 4 Ch 3, 2 dc in ch-3 sp, ch 1 *3 dc in
next ch-3 sp, ch 1. Rep from * around. Join
rnd with sl st in top of beg-ch. 45 dc + 15
ch-1 sps
Rnd 5 Ch 5, *3 dc in next ch-1 sp, ch 2. Rep
from * to last st, 2 dc in last sc. Join rnd
with sl st in 3rd ch of beg-ch. 45 dc + 15
ch-2 sps
Rnd 6 Sl st across to first ch-2 sp, ch 3, 2
dc in same ch-2 sp, ch 2,*3 dc in next ch-2
sp,ch 3. Rep from * around. Join rnd with sl
st in 3rd ch of beg-ch. 45 dc + 15 ch-3 sps
Rnds 7 – 10 Rep Rnd 6.

Band
Rnd 1 Ch 2 (counts as 1 hdc), hdc around
placing 1 hdc in each dc and 2 hdc in each
ch-3 sp. Join rnd with sl st in top of beg-ch.
76 hdc counting ch-2
Rnds 2 & 3 Ch 2 (does not count as 1 hdc),
*FPhdc, BPhdc; rep from * around. Join rnd
with sl st in top of beg-ch.
End off.

Finishing
Weave in ends.

brimming over

Yarn [4]
Sheep(ish) by Vickie Howell by Bernat
3oz/85g skeins, each approx 167yd/153m
(acrylic/wool)
• 1 skein in Grey(ish) #0003

Needles
Size H/8 (5.0mm) crochet hook OR SIZE
NEEDED TO OBTAIN GAUGE

Additional
Tapestry needle
1 sheet of plastic canvas

Measurements
9"/23cm tall x 24"/61cm in diameter
slightly stretched

Gauge
12 sts and 10 rows to 4"/10cm over hdc
TAKE TIME TO CHECK YOUR GAUGE.

Notes
Ch-3 counts as 1 dc unless otherwise
noted.
Ch-2 does not count as 1 hdc in Body; it
does count as 1 hdc in Brim Flap.

Stitch Glossary
FPdc = front post double crochet
BPdc = back post double crochet

Directions

Crown
Ch 4, join into ring with sl st in 1st ch.

Rnd 1 Ch 3 (counts as 1 dc), 10 dc in ring.
Join rnd with sl st in top of beg-ch. 11 dc

Rnd 2 Ch 3, dc in same st as sl st, 2 dc in
each dc around. 22 dc

Rnd 3 Ch 3, dc in same st as sl st, dc in
next dc *2 dc in next dc, dc in next dc. Rep
from * around. Join rnd with sl st in top of
beg-ch. 33 sts

Rnd 4 Ch 3, dc in same st as sl st, dc in
each of next 2 dc, *2 dc in next dc, dc in
each of next2 dc. Rep from * around. Join
rnd with sl st in top of beg-ch. 44 dc

Rnd 5 Ch 3, dc in same st as sl st, dc in
each of next 3 dc, *2 dc in next dc, dc in
each of next 3 dc. Rep from * around. Join
rnd with sl st in top of beg-ch. 55 sts

Rnd 6 Ch 3, dc in same st as sl st, dc in
each of next 4 dc,* 2 dc in next dc, dc in
each of next 4 dc. Rep from * around. Join
rnd with sl st in top of beg-ch. 66 sts

Body
Rnds 1-8 Ch 3 (does not count as dc),
*FPdc, BPdc; rep from * around. Join rnd
with sl st in top of beg-ch.

Rnds 9 & 10 Ch 2, hdc in each dc around.
Join rnd with l st in top of beg-ch.
End off.

Brim flap
Count 9 sts from center. Join yarn with a
sl st.

Row 1 Ch 2 (counts as hdc), hdc in each of
next 17 sts. Ch 2, turn. 18 sts

Row 2-8 Hdc in each hdc across. Ch 2, turn.
Do not ch 2 after Row 8, end off.

Finishing
Using template as a guide, cut out brim
piece from plastic canvas. Fold brim flap
over plastic piece as snugly as possible so
that brim curves into shape. Seam closed
with tapestry needle.

Weave in ends.

Brim Template

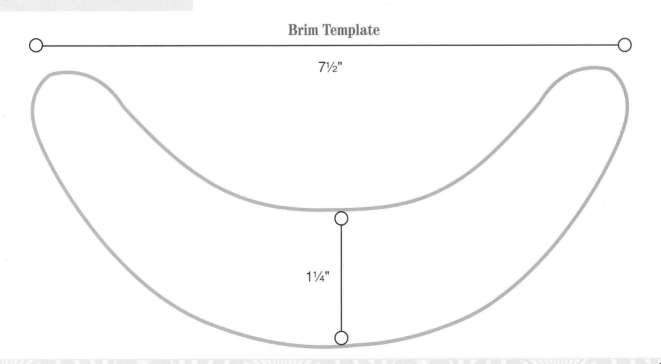

7½"

1¼"

my notes